C

Scholastic Children's Books,
Commonwealth House, 1 – 19 New Oxford Street, London WC1A 1NU
a division of Scholastic Limited
London – New York – Toronto – Sydney – Auckland
Published by Scholastic Limited Copyright © Scholastic Limited 1997
Text by Deri Robins
All rights reserved
ISBN 0 590 19408 9
Printed in Hong Kong
10 9 8 7 6 5 4 3 2 1

Welcome to your very own Guide for Girls!

Growing up is all about new CHOICES and new INTERESTS. You're probably starting to get pretty interested in things like fashion and beauty, and might be wondering where to start.

Maybe you'd love to give your bedroom a new look, and need a few suggestions to get you going. Top Tips for Girls is here to help – definitely not to tell you how to lead your life, but to give you some really useful advice.

There's also some handy hints on CHOOSING PETS, making your POCKET MONEY stretch a little bit further, and how to 'read' other people's BODY LANGUAGE. You can also discover whether you're true to your STAR SIGN, and what your DOODLES reveal about your PERSONALITY.

Beauty Basics

The old saying is absolutely true – real beauty comes from within! It all starts with eating well, taking the right kind of exercise, and keeping your skin and hair clean and shining.

Healthy eating makes you look and feel great. Here are some basic dos and don'ts:

DO . . .

. . . eat some fresh fruit and vegetables every day.

. . . grab a handful of nuts and raisins as a snack rather than crisps and biscuits.

. . . drink half-fat rather than full-fat milk.

. . . eat whole-wheat bread rather than white bread, and sugar free muesli rather than sugary cereals.

DON'T

. . . eat too many sweets, cakes or chocolates. You don't have to cut them out altogether – just make them an occasional treat.

. . . eat lots of fried foods. Grilled foods are better for you.

. . . drink sweet fizzy drinks like cola. Try mixing fruit juice with sparkling water instead. A glass of water is best of all.

Keeping Fit

It doesn't matter what shape you are – it's the shape you're in that counts!

Regular exercise will give you bags of energy, a fabulous, toned up body and clear, sparkly eyes. Some of the best forms of exercise are walking (briskly), swimming, skipping, gymnastics, bike riding and dancing – all of which are great fun in their own right.

Good posture's important too. People really notice the way you stand and walk, so hold your head up, pull your shoulders back and keep your tummy in. You'll look happier and more confident – and you'll start to feel that way too!

Your Skin

- For a clear, glowing complexion, wash your face with a non-perfumed soap (baby soap is good) and make sure that you rinse it thoroughly with warm water.

- If your skin feels dry after washing, smooth on a little moisturizer.

- If your skin feels oily, you could try a mild toner. Pour a little on to a damp cotton wool ball, and wipe it gently over your face.

Make-up

It's far more natural to wear light make-up – if you want to wear it at all, as you really don't need to! Older women sometimes wear foundations or powders to make their skin look as young as yours does naturally.

If you want to try make-up, this is all you need to do:
* Tie your hair back with a hair band, then clean and moisturize your face.
* For your lips, you'll need a natural coloured lipstick, a lip brush and some clear lip-gloss. Use the brush to outline the lips, and to fill them in. Blot them lightly with a tissue, and smooth on some gloss.

* Eye make-up is fun for parties and special occasions. Whatever the colour of your eyes, neutral colours like browns, pinky browns and greys are far more flattering than bright blues, greens or purples.

Brush a light shade all over the lids.

Blend a darker shade over the outer half of the lids and sockets.

Using a soft kohl pencil, draw a fine line around the eyelids. Smudge gently.

Brush a light coat of mascara over the top lashes, then over the bottom ones. Use a clean mascara brush or an eyelash brush to separate the lashes, to make them look more natural. You can also use the brush to neaten your eyebrows.

Smile!

A dazzling smile begins with brushing your teeth thoroughly every morning and before going to bed. A quick brush after eating sweets or fizzy drinks is a good idea too. Visit your dentist twice a year – if you look after your teeth, you may never need fillings.

Scientists have proved that smiling and laughing release 'happy hormones' into the body, which can actually make you feel more cheerful.

Your Hair

Whether you wear your hair short or long, it'll look brilliant if you really take care of it!

The massive range of shampoos in the shops can seem confusing – and expensive! Try not to be taken in by TV and magazine adverts – all you need is a simple, mild shampoo. Always rinse every trace of the suds from your hair, using cool water for extra shine.

* If your hair is oily, wash it a bit more often. You'll soon work out how many times is right for you.

* If your hair or scalp is very dry, try massaging in a little olive or almond oil about 30 minutes before washing.

* Let your hair dry naturally if you can – blow drying is bad for your hair. If you do want to use a dryer, then wait until your hair is nearly dry before styling.

* Don't tie your hair back with elastic bands, or the ends will split. The 'scrunchie' on page nine is ideal.

Styling Ideas

If you take care of your hair and have it trimmed regularly, it'll look great however you wear it.

A basic cut can be dressed up in all sorts of ways.

✔ *Use hair gel to slick back short hair. Coloured gels are fun for special occasions.*

✔ Sweep hair back over the ears, and pin with slides or combs.

✔ *For a plait with a difference, tie a long ribbon around the hair to make a pony tail, then make a plait using the tails of the ribbon to tie the end of the plait in a bow.*

✔ Try making lots of tiny plaits, and tie beads onto the ends with coloured thread.

✔ A french plait looks wonderful – ask a friend to help.

❀ *Gather a small section of hair from the top of your head, and divide into three.*

❀ *Start plaiting the hair – but add extra sections from the right and left as you do so.*

❀ *Carry on plaiting until the hair is taken up into the braid. Fasten the ends as before.*

✔ For a soft, pretty look, divide your hair into two at the back. Twist each side into a roll, and fasten at the nape of the neck with a band.

✔ Try wrapping lengths of wool, ribbon or silk around strands of hair, making sure that the hair is completely covered. Thread the braids with coloured beads for extra effect.

✔ Use braiding to make a 'false hairpiece' if you have a short hairstyle. Overlap the strand of hair with a second piece of thread, and keep twisting.

Here are some quick and easy hair accessories to stick and sew – they make brilliant presents too!

Scrunchie

❥ For each scrunchie, you'll need a scrap of fabric measuring 25 X 5 cm, a piece of elastic measuring 25 cm, a needle and thread.

❥ *Fold the fabric in half, and sew up the long side.*

❥ *Turn it inside out, and push the elastic through the middle.*

❥ *Knot the elastic, and push the ends inside the fabric tube.*

❥ *Sew up the ends of the fabric neatly.*

Gorgeous Grips

Plain metal slides can be bought from craft shops. You could also by cheap plastic covered slides from the chemist.

● Find pretty beads and fake gems in craft shops, and glue these to the slide. Add glitter for a sparkling party look.

● Tie big bows from scraps of silk or velvet. Cut a short strip to go round the middle, and glue this to the slide.

● Buy a fake flower from a florist, and glue it to the slide.

FASHION AND STYLE

Although it's fun to see what the top models are wearing, the most important thing is making the best of yourself by finding a look that suits you. Wishing for someone else's face, figure or colouring is a complete waste of time.

Colours

Have you ever wondered why the lime-coloured T-shirt that looks so fantastic on your best friend makes you look washed out? The answer is that different hair and skin colours suit different shades. Here's a simple guide:

FAIR COMPLEXION AND HAIR

* Try Navy and dark blues rather than pastel shades.
* Soft greens and turquoise are flattering. So are shades of yellow and gold.
* Red or dusty pink can look great!

BROWN/BLACK HAIR AND SKIN

*Girls with dark hair and skin can get away with many exciting and unusual shades –

try plum, maroon, raspberry and lime green.

* White and cream look stunning against dark skin.

* Yellow and coral make a great summer wardrobe.

AUBURN HAIR AND FAIR SKIN

* All shades of green look wonderful. So do greeny-blues, and light pastel blue.

* Grey with touches of white looks cool.

* Dusky pink looks great. So do natural colours such as beige and brown.

MEDIUM/LIGHT BROWN HAIR AND FAIR SKIN

* Heathery colours – mossy green, mustard and the colour of autumn leaves all look great. So do darker shades of green.

* Deep ocean blues, lilac and turquoise all work well – especially with blue eyes.

* Yellow and peach look good in the summer, with a light tan.

Remember – everyone is different. Wear colours that you feel good in.

Flatter your shape

- Did you know that the pattern and shape of your clothes can change the way you look?

* If you're tall and thin, horizontal stripes will make your figure seem fuller. Avoid long, straight dresses – go for full skirts or slightly baggy trousers, and pull them in at the waist.

* If you want to look a bit slimmer, you could wear vertical stripes. Long shirts, jumpers or shift dresses are flattering too. Plain colours or small print are better than big, bright designs.

FASHION BUDGET

Try to build up a good, basic wardrobe – jeans, T-shirts and big, baggy shirts are classics that never seem to go out of fashion.

* If you're dying for the latest look, but can't afford the whole outfit, buy some new accessories instead. The right belt, necklace, scarf or hat will make all the difference.

* Check out your local charity shops, jumble sales and car boot sales. You can often find good quality clothes at very cheap prices.

* Unless your dad has seriously bad taste, see if you can borrow some of his shirts and jumpers. These can look great over a pair of thick tights or leggings.

* Invite your friends over to a clothes-swapping party. That bright orange shirt that makes you feel like a tangerine may be the very thing your friend wants – while you've always hankered after the silver lurex jumper that doesn't fit her these days.

* Breathe new life into old clothes by sewing on trimmings such as huge, outsize buttons, ribbons, lace, beads or sequins.

* Jazz up plain clothes and trainers with fabric paints or crayons. If you're not much good at drawing, try printing – cut simple shapes from thick cardboard, or from half a potato. Dip into the paint, and press onto the fabric.

* TIE-DYE is a brilliant and groovy way to make your clothes very trendy! Use cold water dye to give an old cotton t-shirt or leggings the treatment:

✽ *Tie the clothes into small clumps with thread.*
✽ *Put them in a bucket filled with water mixed with dye (check the instructions on the packet). Leave for about an hour.*
✽ *Rinse in cold water, squeeze, and leave to dry. Ask an adult to iron out the wrinkles when the clothes are dry.*

Making Marvellous Jewellery

Jewellery making is great fun and will save you money too! Special fastenings for earrings, necklaces and badges, called 'findings' can be bought quite cheaply from craft shops.

Necklaces

You can buy beads from craft shops – or be inventive and make your own.

* Cut long triangles from paper. Cover both sides with PVA glue, then roll them round a knitting needle. Paint and varnish the beads when dry, and thread onto some strong cotton. Knot the ends together.

* Dried leaves and seeds make natural looking 'beads'. You can also use shells – ask an adult to help you make the holes.

* Raid the food cupboard! Pasta tubes can be painted silver and gold, while liquorice allsorts look delicious just as they are (but they might get a bit sticky after a while!).

* Roll self-hardening clay into beads – they can be round, oval, square, or any shape you like! Push a knitting needle through the middle of the beads, and leave to dry before painting or varnishing.

Excellent Earrings

* Thread beads onto hoops, or the kind of findings used for pierced ears.

* Mould shapes from self-hardening clay. Leave to dry, then paint and varnish. These can be glued to clip-on earrings; if you want to use pierced-ear findings, then push the pins into the clay before it dries.

Brilliant Badges, Brooches and Bracelets

* Roll out some self-hardening clay, and cut out a shape (heart, diamond, star – whatever you like!) with a knife. Leave to dry, then paint your design and varnish. Glue a badge finding to the back.

* Make a simple friendship bracelet from three pieces of different-coloured thread, each about 30cm long. Make a knot at one end, then plait the threads together. Make a knot at the other end, and add beads for extra decoration.

How to Survive When You're Flat Broke

Here are some good ideas for making your allowance stretch that little bit further.

* Earn some extra cash. Your parents may agree to pay you to wash the car, weed the garden, clean out the budgie cage, help your younger brother and sister with homework, do the washing up, or keep your room tidy. But if they don't...

Collect any good-quality clothes, books and records you don't want, and sell them to a second hand shop. Or get some friends together and ask an adult to drive you to a car boot sale – your parents may let you sell their old junk too (especially if you agree to give half the money to charity).

* Have a swap party (see page 14). Old clothes, books, cassettes, CDs, magazines, video's and games are all brilliant to swap.

* Learn to budget. Keep a note of your weekly spending – sweets, magazines, etc. If you spend more than you get in pocket money, it's time to make some cutbacks – especially if you're saving for something special.

Lots of activities cost nothing or next to nothing.
Here are just a few ideas:

❑ Ask if you can have a sleepover party, and share the cost of hiring a couple of videos with your friends. (You might be able to persuade your parents to supply the pizza and popcorn).

✐ Hold a knockout Scrabble/Twister/computer games tournament with your class at school.

★ Start a collection of old stamps, keys, buttons, comics or anything else that people throw away – it might be worth something one day!

☛ Sow some seeds (flowers, herbs – even tomatoes) in a window box, or garden if you have one, and watch them grow!

✐ Get together with your friends, and compile a 'best ever' music collection by taping everyone's favourite tracks on to one tape.

✎ Make friends with someone in a different country. Lots of magazines have addresses of pen-pal organisations.

$ Plan a makeover for your bedroom (see pages 19–21).

✐ Get involved with a local charity. If you're interested in animals, wildlife and the environment, write to groups like Greenpeace and Friends of the Earth to see how you could help.

Making Over Your Room

If you can't stand another day of looking at the cute bunny wallpaper you've had since you were five, it's time to make some changes. . .

The first thing to do is to clear out all your old rubbish. Fill carrier bags with things that can be sold/given to charity/recycled, and throw everything else in a bin.

Up the Wall

* Paint the walls a new colour! White and cream look bright and fresh; most shades of blue look cool and make a small room look bigger; greens are calm and restful; reds and pinks are warm and cosy, and a yellow room will always be full of sunshine – even when it's pouring with rain outside!

* You can also stencil your walls, using small trial pots of emulsion from DIY shops:
Draw a design on some thin card, and ask an adult to cut out the holes with a craft knife. Dip a stencilling brush in the paint, and dab it over the stencil. The brush should be almost dry. If it's wet, the paint will leak under the stencil.

Gold stars, suns and moons look great on dark walls or ceilings.

Choose a simple pattern, and repeat it around the top, bottom or middle of the room.

Look through books and magazines for shapes to trace or copy.
Use fabric paint to make matching designs on duvet covers, pillowcases and curtains!

* Try writing to the tourist departments of foreign embassies for posters of faraway places; film distributors and video hire shops for movie posters, and record companies for posters advertising their latest releases.

* Use photos from magazines to turn one wall into a giant collage. Overlap all the pictures, so that there aren't any gaps in between.

* Glue a big piece of corrugated card or polystyrene to some bright material to make a pinboard. Make two small holes near the top of the board, thread with string, and hang on the wall. Or, hang up a piece of garden netting, and fix on your favourite bits and pieces with clothes pegs – great for a room with a seaside theme!

* Load your camera with black and white film, and take lots of arty-looking photos of your pets, friends, local buildings, etc. Frame the best ones.

Fabulous Furniture

* Old bits of furniture can be found in junk shops, jumble sales and even skips. A coat of gloss paint in the latest pastel shades will make almost everything look terrific.

* Make cushion covers from fake fur for a fun '60s look.

* A pile of bricks and some planks of wood make an instant bookcase. You can also knock the bottom out of a wooden box, to make shelves for displaying a collection.

* Paint old boxes and baskets, and use them to stash your junk.

Star Signs

ARIES (The Ram)

March 21st – April 20th

People born under the sign of the ram have quick
minds, bags of energy and a natural talent for leadership.
Impatient Arians aren't very good at keeping their
temper, but never bear a grudge for long!

Colour: Red   Birthstones: Diamond, ruby

Famous Arians: Diana Ross, Emma Thomson, Damon Albarn

TAURUS (The Bull)

April 21st – May 20th

Taureans are usually easy-going, but can be
very determined if necessary! Practical, responsible
and reliable, they make good and loyal friends.

Colours: Green, pink

Birth stones: Emerald, topaz

Famous Taureans: Cher,
Michelle Pfeiffer, Jack Nicholson

GEMINI (The Twins)

May 22nd – June 21st

It's not easy to know where you stand with someone
born under the sign of the twins. Lively, sociable
Gemini loves change and novelty, and is
easily the most fickle sign of the zodiac!

Colours: Yellow and white

Birthstone: Garnet

Famous Geminians: Naomi Campbell,
Benazir Bhutto, Johnny Depp

22

CANCER (The Crab)

June 21st – July 21st

Cancerians are kind, home-loving and sensitive – the sort that's always there with a tissue and sympathy when you need them. Their feelings are easily hurt, however, and it's not difficult to send them scuttling back into their shell.

Colours: Violet, white

Birthstones: Pearl, moonstone

Famous Cancerians: Princess Diana, Harrison Ford, George Michael

LEO (The Lion)

July 22nd – August 21st

People born under the sign of the lion are adventurous, brave, warm-hearted and generous to a fault. Leo hates to be ignored, and needs lots of praise and attention.

Colours: Fiery reds, gold, purple

Birthstone: Ruby, topaz

Famous Leos: Madonna, Robert de Niro, Christian Slater

VIRGO (The Virgin)

August 22nd – September 22nd

Neat, honest, organised and efficient, Virgo's the one to ask if you want a job well done. Virgo makes a caring, helpful friend. However, their high standards can sometimes make them over-critical of others.

Colours: Grey, navy and brown

Birthstone: Agate

Famous Virgoans: Claudia Shiffer, Liam Gallagher, Keanu Reeves

LIBRA (The Scales)
September 23rd – October 22nd
Librans hate life to be unfair or upsetting and spend a lot of time pouring oil on troubled waters.
They find it very hard to make up their mind – after all, there are two sides to every story. . .
Colours: Pastels and subtle shades
Birthstones: Opal, zircon
Famous Librans: Hilary Clinton, Dawn French, Luke Perry

SCORPIO (The Scorpion)
October 23rd – November 22nd
Scorpios have keen judgement, and make up their minds very quickly. They never do things by halves, and either like or dislike other people very strongly. Not surprisingly, other people often feel the same way about them!
Colours: Black and other dark colours
Birthstone: Topaz
Famous Scorpios: Julia Roberts, Yasmin Le Bon, Leonardo DiCaprio

SAGITTARIUS (The Archer)
November 22nd – December 22nd
Sagittarians are generous, kind and honest, and good at seeing other people's points of view. Their lively wit and good nature makes them great company to be with.
Colours: Purple, deep blue
Birthstone: Amethyst
Famous Sagittarians: Sinead O'Connor, Tina Turner, Brad Pitt

CAPRICORN (The Goat)

December 21st – January 19th

Capricorns are ambitious, energetic and patient – if they set themselves a goal they are likely to reach it. They sometimes find it hard to make friends, but when they do they are friends for life.

Colour: Black

Birthstone: Aquamarine, Jet

Famous Capricorns: Kate Moss, Helena Christensen, David Bowie

AQUARIUS (The Water Carrier)

January 20th – February 18th

Aquarians love freedom and independence. They can make warm and lasting friend ships, but they're often more interested in helping good causes then any one person in particular.

Colour: Electric blue

Birthstone: Sapphire

Famous Aquarians: Mia Farrow, Robbie Williams, John Travolta

PISCES (The Fish)

February 19th – March 20th

Pisceans are romantic, sensitive, gifted and artistic. They have gentle, dreamy natures and are generous and helpful – but don't turn to the fish if you need someone to help you make a decision!

Colours: Sea green, mauve and grey

Birthstone: Amethyst, moonstone

Famous Pisceans: Cindy Crawford, Drew Barrymore, Bruce Willis

PETMANIA

So you're thinking of getting a pet? Here are some useful things to know before you rush off to buy a feathered, finned or furry friend. . .

Dogs

A dog will love you to bits, even when the rest of the world has turned against you – but in return it needs a lot of care and attention. Someone will have to take it for a walk at least once a day, and look after it when you're at school and away on holiday. You really need to have parents that are as dog crazy as you are for this to work.

Cats

Cats are easier than dogs. They don't need walking, they keep themselves clean, and won't pine too much if you go away for the weekend (as long as you've organised someone to come in and feed them). Bear in mind that all kittens are completely insane, and will ruth-lessly shred curtains, furniture and hands until they grow older and calm down a bit.

Rabbits

Rabbits can live indoors, but it's more usual to keep them in a hutch in the garden. It doesn't cost much to feed them and they look cute and fluffy, but some bite!

Hamsters

Hamsters like to sleep in the day, and get very bad-tempered when you wake them up. Still, they're very pretty, and there are lots of amusing things you can buy to exercise them in (including a plastic racing car that's powered by the hamster racing round in a special wheel).

Fish

Goldfish are cheap to keep, as you don't need any special equipment – a wide, clear bowl and tap water will be fine. Tropical fish are definitely more interesting, but they're more expensive to keep. Their tanks need to be kept at exactly the right temperature, and must be fitted with an air pump. Even then, the whole collection can easily be wiped out by some mysterious disease.

Budgie

If you're going to keep a budgie, buy it plenty of toys – ladders, swings, mirrors and bells – to make up for the boredom of being stuck in a cage all day. If you're hoping to teach it to talk, make sure that it's under three months old when you buy it.

Doodling

You may already know that your handwriting can reveal your hidden character – but did you know that your doodles can give you away too? Check the pad by the phone to uncover the inner secrets of your personality. . .

Filler-inner
If you fill in the letters in a name or message, you hate to see anything wasted.
Filled-in patterns can mean that the doodler is worrying about something.

Squiggler
Lots of flourishes can mean you're artistic, but a bit of a show-off. . .

. . . but regular patterns show a careful, practical personality.

Boxes
If you draw boxes inside boxes, you have a very clear idea of what you want from life.

Hearts
You're in love with love!

Arrows and ladders
You know what you want – and intend to get it!

Houses
Drawing a house means that you like to feel safe and secure. If you draw a path, it means that you don't feel that way at the moment.

Birds
You have an affectionate nature.

Faces
Faces turned to the left means you are shy and reserved. A face turned to the right means that you are sure of yourself, but sometimes forget about other people's feelings. A full face means a happy, friendly nature – unless of course the face if wearing a fierce or unhappy expression!

£££ signs
Money is very much on your mind at the moment.

Webs
You may be looking for the answer to a difficult problem – the web shows that you feel trapped.

Animals
You long to feel that you fit in, and hate arguments.

Planes, boats and trains
You may long to travel to distant places – or just to try out some new ideas or hobbies.

BODY LANGUAGE

You can tell at lot about the way someone's feeling before they even open their mouth. Here's how to listen in!

STANDING AND SITTING

Standing with shoulders back and head held high: "I feel confident and sure of myself."

A hunched, slouched posture with head held down: "I feel unsure and anxious."

Pointing the body towards a new person joining a group: "You're welcome to join us."

Keeping the body pointed away: "We don't want you to join this conversation."

Straddling a chair: "I want to take control."

Leaning back in a chair with hands behind the head: "I'm cleverer than you!"

Legs tightly held together or tightly crossed:
"I feel unfriendly/nervous."

EYE CONTACT

A sideways look with raised eyebrows:
"I am interested in you."

A sideways look with eyebrows down:
"I do not approve of you."

ARMS AND HANDS

Arms crossed across the body:
"I feel nervous and unsure."

Open palms and hands:
"I feel relaxed, and have an open mind."

TALKING. . .

Covering mouth while talking:
"I am not telling the truth."

Holding a steady gaze:
"I am confident of myself."

Eyes averted:
"I am nervous/cannot be trusted."

Eyes closed:
"I feel superior to you."

LISTENING

Picking fluff from clothes/scratching neck:
"I don't agree with what you're saying."

Rubbing back of neck:
"I find you a pain in the neck."

Rubbing ear:
"I don't want to hear any more."

Using hand to support the head:
"I'm bored!